What Others Are Saying

"Your Magic is a powerful story that sparks inspiration and confidence in children. As an adult, I was also reminded of my own magic while reading. The combination of beautiful illustrations and Kylee's descriptive examples encourage children with different skill sets and backgrounds to find their own magic through this book. I highly recommend it for children and parents to reconnect with the magic that's always been inside of them."
- Jaclyn Gallo, author and mental health advocate

"Your Magic will capture young readers with its colorful pages and catchy rhymes. It does a spectacular job featuring people from all areas and walks of life and does so in a subtle way. The overarching message drives home the fact that what sets us apart is often what makes us special, strong, and resilient, things we all desire for our children."
- Beth Leipholtz, Author of *The ABCs of Inclusion*

"Such a profound and timely message. This book creates space for all of today's youth despite their age, race, color, gender, or unique talent. A gift that offers a magical space to find one's self. Well-written and vibrant graphics pull the readers into the world of magic that this work so beautifully unfolds."
- Talisa Lavarry, TedX & Keynote Speaker, America's Anti-Racism Coach, Author

Your Magic

Published by Bell Asteri Publishing & Enterprises, LLC
209 West 2nd Street #177
Fort Worth TX 76102
www.bellasteri.com

Published in the United States of America

ISBN: 978-1-957604-33-6 (hardback)
ISBN: 978-1-957604-34-3 (paperback)
ISBN: 978-1-957604-35-0 (electronic book)

for those

fearless

enough to share their

✶ M A G I C ✶

with this BIG

⸫BRIGHT⸫

world ♡

In a tiny little corner,
deep inside your heart,
lives a piece of you called your magic
and it's what sets you apart.

It's smaller than a snowflake
and twinkles like a star.
It's the guiding light inside you
that makes you who you are.

What makes your magic sparkle
is what makes you, you.
It's your uniqueness and individuality
and all the special things you do.

It's what makes you happy
and makes you laugh or cry.
It's how you view the world
and you couldn't lose it if you tried.

Everyone's magic is specific
and might not be the same.
There will be similarities that connect you
but it's your own magic to proclaim!

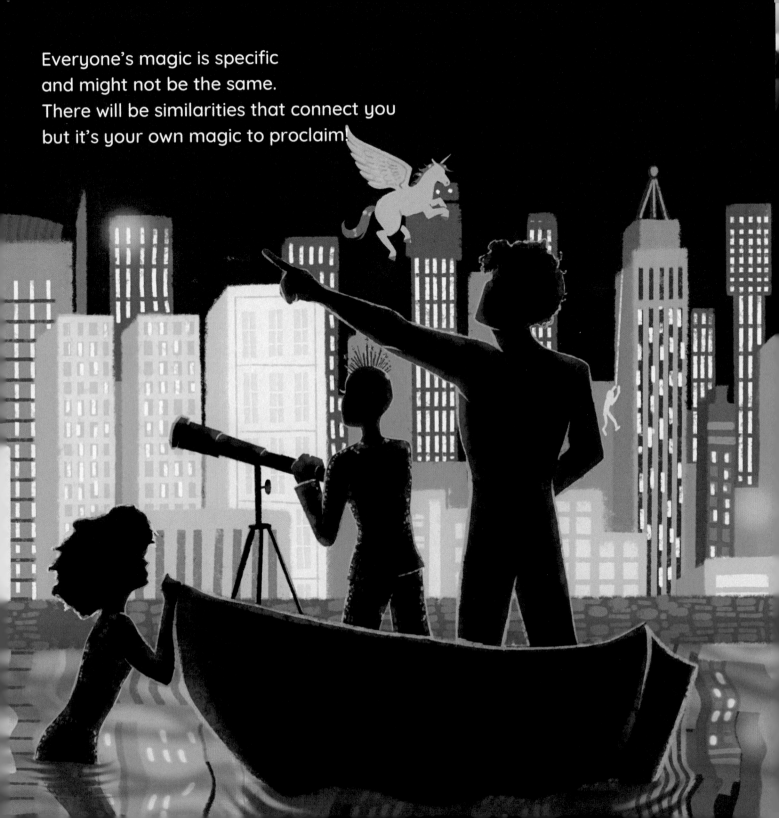

Your magic may be your leadership
and your ability to guide a team,
the way you share your voice,
and make others feel seen.

Your magic may be your empathy,
and your ability to relate and understand.

Your magic may be your resourcefulness
and how you always lend a helping hand.

Your magic may be your cunning mind
that deciphers puzzles and problem solves,
how you give everyone a space to speak,
with no problem you can't resolve.

Your magic may be your artistry,
how you bring color to the room,
being the star of the show,
or helping others bloom.

Your magic may be your light
that always finds a way
to brighten up every dark situation
even when you feel afraid.

How you fill a room with laughter,
or listen to understand,
how you bring people together
in a way that only you can.

The curiosity that excites you,
how you always want to know more,
the bravery that your heart holds
that dares you to explore.

Maybe it's your super speed
and how far and fast you'll go
or perhaps it's your resilience
to pivot, change and grow.

It's magic to bring people together
and lead them to a common goal,
or gluing the pieces back together
and helping them feel whole.

What makes you magical may be your vision, and
using your intuition as your guide,
or connecting with those around you
and the friendships by your side.

Or perhaps it's your strength,
in your heart, body, and mind.
It's the way you always want to help
or take note to always be kind.

Your magic may be your passion
that reliably strikes a spark,

or the fearlessness that lights a path,
when other roads seem dark.

How you quiet the world to focus,
or courageously use your voice,
how you share your heart's song with the world,
how thoughtfully you make a choice.

The way you ask for help when you need it,
especially when it's not easy for you to do,
how you encourage others to be themselves
simply by being yourself too.

The way you love and
how you care,
or your spirit,
daring and bold,

your magic is a
dazzling wonder
and truly something
to behold.

It's how you see the world for what it could be and not simply for what it is right now.

Your magic is the passion that will help you build it even if you're not exactly quite sure how.

When your magic feels dimmed -- because it may --
and you can't hear its special song,
take a moment to look inside you,
because your magic has been there all along.

Steady your hands and take a deep breath,
close your eyes, and let yourself feel
the little piece deep inside your heart,
because that's the magic that's truly real.

You have your magic because you are magic,
from the top of your head to deep inside your bones,
and as long as you have you,
you are never truly alone.

But somehow I have a funny feeling
that your magic is not to hide

and sharing it will guide you
to others who will always be by your side.

Now as you face this big brave world,
remember that deep inside your heart,
lives a little piece of you called your magic
and it's what sets you apart.

To enhance the reader's experience of reading Your Magic and delve deeper into self-reflection, these questions can be used as prompts to encourage personal exploration and connection to the book's themes, no matter what the reader's age is.

1. **Three words to describe yourself:** Encourage readers to think about their own unique qualities and select three words that best represent who they are. This exercise allows them to embrace their individuality and relate to the characters in the book.

2. **Color and fashion sense:** Ask readers to envision the color they would wear and describe their fashion sense. Prompt them to reflect on their personal style and why they are drawn to specific colors or fashion choices. This encourages self-expression and understanding of their own tastes.

3. **Favorite qualities to share:** Encourage readers to identify their favorite qualities that they enjoy sharing with others. This helps them recognize their strengths and the positive attributes they bring to relationships and interactions. Similarly, prompt them to reflect on qualities that they might not favor and explore why that might be the case.

4. **Presenting oneself to the world:** Ask readers to consider how they currently present themselves to the world and how they aspire to present themselves. This question encourages self-reflection on personal growth, authenticity, and the image they want to project.

5. **Representation in the media:** Inquire about how readers have seen themselves represented in the media. This prompts them to reflect on diversity, inclusion, and the importance of representation in shaping identity and self-perception.

6. **Boosting confidence:** Prompt readers to explore what helps them feel more confident. This question encourages them to identify and celebrate the factors or activities that empower them, building self-assurance and resilience.

By engaging with these questions, readers can deepen their connection to the themes explored in "Your Magic" and gain a greater understanding of themselves, their uniqueness, and their journey of self-discovery.

An infinite amount of "thank you's" are required for taking this book from a dream to a dream come true.

Thank you to my amazing team at Bell Asteri, especially Dana-Susan Crews, for taking a chance on me, on us, and on this story. Thank you to our talented illustrator and human sunshine, Estella Patrick, for making these characters come to life so beautifully. Thank you to Maddi Stanton-Johnson, Anna Cahill, and the Original Character Committee Members for loving these characters as much as I do, giving them the care, attention, and ability to exist in the way they deserve. Thank you to Omoanatse McArthur for constantly leading our organization to be a part of true transformational change and helping us go further with heart.

Thank you to my parents, Carol and Paul, for wholeheartedly believing in me and giving me the most beautiful life. I hope to be a sliver of who you are when I grow up. To my sisters, Rosie and Dani, for being my best friends first and my confidants always. You are both what I always wished for. Thank you to my grandparents Florence and Edward for being my first friends and for being a guiding light leading me to A Moment of Magic.

Thank you to my husband, Matthew, who saw a light in me long before I ever saw it in myself, for making me better every single day, and for creating our own real life fairytale. I am so grateful for this marvelous adventure we are on together. Thank you for countless conversations, your incredible patience, and your steadfast belief. Thank you to Riggins, too.

Thank you to my incredible community, from supporters, to mentors, to teachers, to friends, and family. You give the people of Bedford Falls a run for their money. Thank you for making every place I have been privileged to be feel like home and for supporting these big, wild dreams.

Thank you to the all of the many places I pulled inspiration and kept me company during so many of life's moments, including my beloved fairytales, New York City, and (of course) Taylor Swift.

Thank you to the countless children and volunteers who inspired these characters, who allowed us to infuse their own life stories into who these characters grew to be, and for helping them jump off the page and into the real world where they make a true difference every single day.

This story is for you.

About Your Magic

"Your Magic" is a captivating children's book that takes readers on a whimsical journey into the power of self-discovery and embracing one's uniqueness. In a world where magic is synonymous with the special qualities that make us who we are, readers are introduced to a vibrant cast of over 30 diverse and inclusive characters. These characters, co-created with A Moment of Magic's volunteers and the children they serve, represent the multifaceted nature of humanity and inspire young readers to see themselves as the heroes of their own stories.

As readers embark on a journey of self-discovery alongside the book's endearing characters, they learn that everyone's magic is distinctive and deserves to be celebrated. "Your Magic" encourages readers to embrace their true selves, find joy in their individuality, and recognize the magic within. With its uplifting message and enchanting illustrations, this book ignites the imagination, fosters self-confidence, and reminds us all that embracing our unique magic can lead to extraordinary adventures.

About A Moment of Magic

A Moment of Magic is a nonprofit organization founded in 2014 in a college dorm room with the mission to bring joy and magic to children facing medical challenges. In November 2016, a touch of magic propelled A Moment of Magic's story to viral status, accumulating over 65 million views worldwide. This international recognition served as a catalyst for the organization, allowing it to be embraced by colleges and universities across the United States. Presently, A Moment of Magic engages over 1,300 college student volunteers from more than 30 institutions, partnering with 300+ hospitals and nonprofits to provide imaginative programs for over 100,000 children.

Through their network of dedicated college student volunteers, A Moment of Magic provides character visits, hospital programs, and therapeutic play experiences to support children in hospitals and other medical facilities, fostering hope, resilience, and a sense of normalcy during difficult times, always reminding children to be brave, strong, and fearless.

You can learn more about A Moment of Magic at amomentofmagic.org

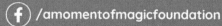

📷 @momentofmagicfoundation   ♪ @momentofmagicfoundation

🐦 @_momentofmagic   f /amomentofmagicfoundation

About the Author

Kylee McGrane-Zarnoch is the Founder and Executive Director of A Moment of Magic Foundation, a dedicated mental health advocate, and an influential content creator. A wholehearted believer in the powers of laughter, friendship, and imagination, Kylee founded A Moment of Magic as a college sophomore and has helped build the organization to where it is today. Kylee's passion, dedication, and impact have garnered global recognition, and she continues to inspire others with her advocacy for mental health, the power of vulnerability, and the pursuit of big dreams. She currently lives in New York City with her husband, Matthew, and their delightfully fluffy puppy, Riggins. Rumor has it, she has never refused a cup of coffee in her life.

Find her online:
kyleelauren.com

@kyleelauren   @kyylauren

@kyleelauren   /kyleelaurenm

About the Illustrator

Estella Patrick was in and out of the hospital at a young age after being born with a congenital spinal defect. During her difficult time in recovery, she found art as a means of coping and as a source of joy! Since her days in the hospital, she has used her love for art to give back through charities, fundraisers, and now, illustration! Estella's hope is to inspire joy in the hearts of pediatric hospital patients through the same artistic creativity that once helped her.

@alleste_kirtap & @alletses_art

Made in the USA
Middletown, DE
19 September 2024

61167152R00020